A Greater Revelation of Jesus and The Power of the Work of the Cross

By
Pastor Mark Pulley

Copyright © 2014 by Mark Pulley

All rights reserved

Printed in the United States of America

International Standard Book Number:

978-1-888081-08-4

This book or parts thereof may not be

reproduced in any form without prior written permission from the author

Published by

GOOD NEWS FELLOWSHIP MINISTRIES

220 Sleepy Creek Rd.

Macon, GA 31210

Phone: (478) 757-8071

Table of Contents

1. Introduction.. 4
2. Jesus Fulfilled All the Law... 5
3. As Jesus Was Crucified We Were Justified................. 12
4. Your are Qualified... 20
5. You are God's Temple... 23
6. Satan a Defeated Foe... 28
7. Prayer Becomes a Guarantee..................................... 32
8. By Grace Through Faith.. 38
9. When Jesus was Resurrected I Received New Life..... 43
10. Stand and Trust... 48
11. A Full Supply.. 52
12. When Jesus Was Rejected I Was Grafted In............. 57
13. Fullness of Life.. 61
14. Righteousness Through His Grace............................ 65
15. Jesus Took Every Infirmity.. 71
16. Unbelief... 77
17. Enter His Rest... 82
18. It is Working.. 85
19. New Covenant Praying.. 96

Introduction

Understanding the fullness of what Jesus did on the cross for us is the beginning of our walk with him and it's the beginning of living a life of victory. Without this understanding our faith will not produce the victory that Jesus came to give to us.

My prayer is that as you read this book concerning what Jesus did on the cross for you, that great revelation of the Lord Jesus Christ and His finished works on Calvary will abound in your heart and bring answers to your life; that where you struggled in your faith, that His Word will begin to break through and manifest as you allow the revelation that is in this book to transform your belief system and thinking to become more in line with the new covenant. As we journey together, we will grow together; and remember this, no one has arrived and we are all learning. So as you begin this study, I declare revelation and great grace upon you by the power of the Holy Spirit and in Jesus name.

It is my belief that we as the body of Christ have not tapped into the fullness of what Jesus did on the cross and it is my heart to help all of us to come into that full revelation of the finished works of Jesus.

Chapter 1

Jesus Fulfilled All the Law

Matthew 5:17-18 ESV Do not think that I am come to abolish the law or the prophets; I have not come to abolish them but to fulfill them…not an Iota , nor dot will pass from the law until all is accomplished.

Through the death, burial and resurrection of the Lord Jesus, Jesus fulfilled, accomplished all the law and the prophets. In him, through him, by him all things are done, they are finished.

Galatians 3:13 Christ has redeemed us from the curse of the law…

Jesus redeemed us from the effects of Adams sin and of our sin (those effects are eternal damnation, sickness, disease and poverty). He did this so that verse 14 could be experienced in our lives. That the blessing of Abraham might come upon the gentiles through faith… (in our Lord Jesus Christ)

Colossians 2:14-15 Having wiped out the handwriting of requirements that was against us which were contrary to us and he has taken it out of the way having nailed it to the cross. Having disarmed principalities and powers he made a public spectacle of them triumphing over them in it. (it is the cross)

So when Jesus was crucified on the cross we were justified, acquitted, declared not guilty. It is just as if we never sinned, wow!!!! The sin, its effects, its sentence over us (sickness, disease, fear, poverty), its legal right to afflict us was broken and removed by the Lord Jesus. He took it upon himself, our guilt, our punishment, our curses; He took so that His blessing, His zoe life would be upon us and in Him, all the law of sin was fulfilled. It was cancelled from having damaging effects upon us. Praise the Lord!

We need a greater revelation of this truth and fact, that satan and his demonic powers and all their sin, evil, and curses can no longer control you or intimidate you or master you when you are born again. Jesus broke their power off of us through His work on the cross. He broke the power of sin and its effects which when you are in Christ, no longer has a legal right to you, your life. You have been redeemed, set free through the power of the work of the cross.

Deuteronomy 28:1-14 reveals in part, the blessing of Abraham and yet it demands 100% total obedience to all God says in order to possess and enjoy these blessings. If you are like me, you very seldom are 100% obedient 24/7. Yet, Jesus was a 100% obedient to all the law and the prophets. There was no sin in Him.

I John 3:5 you know that He was manifested to take away our sins (and its effects) and in Him there is no sin. Because of this, Jesus fulfilled Deuteronomy 28: 1-2 so that all the blessings of Abraham would come upon those who are redeemed in Jesus. Not because of anything we have done, but all because of what He did on the cross and his grace that has been given to those who believe in Him. They are ours by grace through faith in Him. They belong to you as your inheritance.

Jesus made a way for you to be blessed with all that God promised Abraham. Jesus fulfilled all the law and the prophets becoming cursed so we could have life and have life to the full (see Galatians 3:13-14 and John

10:10). It's not about what you and I do or don't do, it's about what Jesus did on the cross, and you're accepting His finished works for your total salvation. When this is a reality to you, your struggle will be over. Sin will no longer dominate you. You will not try to work for His blessing. They are His free gift to you.

Whatever sin or infirmity you may be dealing with, know this, Jesus stripped it off its power and has defeated it by nailing it to the cross. He took its legal right to have any influence in your life away from you so that as a believer in Christ, it has to leave your life. It cannot stay. You are His temple, He lives in you and through your faith in Him, through your faith in His blood, through your faith in the finished works of the cross, you can face whatever it is and speak to that mountain and it will obey your faith (Mark 11:23) which is not your faith, but the faith of the Son of God which He deposited inside of you when you were born again (see Galatians 2:20). It doesn't matter if it's heart disease, Alzheimer's, cancer, drug addition, etc., you are already forgiven, set free, healed and delivered by the power of the work of the cross, and your faith in the power of the work of the cross and in Jesus will give you access to your full redemption.

As a believer, we must see that whatever the enemy attacks us with cannot remain. Jesus totally defeated it. When we understand this, a peace, a shalom will come upon you knowing you have the victory, not going to get the victory, but you have the victory because of what Jesus did. See yourself delivered, set free, just receive all He provided for you when He went to the cross taking your sin, your pain, your demons upon Himself. You are delivered; you are redeemed in Jesus name.

You don't have to try to get it; it already belongs to you by the grace of God. Jesus is so awesome; he lovingly suffered so we could be whole. We no longer have to try to believe, say for healing, provision as He has already provided it. He has already provided it all for us on the cross. The blessing of Abraham is yours and this includes everything we will ever need in this life.

We need our spiritual eyes open (Ephesians 1:17-20) to see this truth and to stop praying from a point of trying to get it, to a place it's already mine because of Jesus and His work on the cross. I know this has made a tremendous difference in me. I am no longer trying to reach souls, set the captives free, be healed or prosperous as all these things I already possess. I have them by grace through faith. It is already done and I call them forth in Jesus name!

It's not about waiting on God to do something, it's about putting your faith in Him for all He has already done, and as you do, that supernatural grace and power goes to work on your behalf to manifest in you, to you, for you, and through you what Jesus has already provided.

Matthew 9:29 according to your faith be it unto you. Ephesians 1:7, 11 in Him we have redemption through His blood the forgiveness of sins; according to the riches of His grace… in Him also we have obtained an inheritance…

It's all through Him because of Him, by Him and by grace through faith in Him we have the fullness of redemption. The fullness of redemption means totally forgiven, past, present and future. Totally prosperous in every area of life, totally healed, spirit, soul and body. It is finished, it is a done deal. We no longer have to try to get it, because Jesus fulfilled all the requirements for it and by grace

He gives it to you as a gift. All you have to do is receive Him and receive it in Jesus name.

Chapter 2

As Jesus Was Crucified We Were Justified

Romans 5:18 The free gift came upon all men unto justification and life.

Romans 3:24 Being justified by His grace through redemption in Christ Jesus.

Romans 3:28 Justified by faith.

Romans 5:9 Justified by His blood.

I Corinthians 6:11 Justified in the name of Jesus.

Romans 3:26 Justifier to the one who has faith in Jesus.

Matthew 12:37 By words you shall be justified.

Justified means acquitted, declared not guilty. The act of declaring men free from guilt and acceptable to Him.

We are not justified because of what we do spiritually, meaning we are not justified because we pray one hour per day or because we fast or because we bring our tithes and offerings into the kingdom, or because we degree and confess God's word or because we worship Him and soak in His presence, no, no, no, a thousand times no. We are justified by what He did on the cross and by our faith in what He did by our words of faith of what He did, by faith in the blood He shed so the power of sin that came into the world through Adam would be broken. His blood, his crucifixion destroyed sin and its effects. It no longer has a legal right or even access to our life because we are under the blood, we are under the shadow of the most high (Psalm 91:1) and we are under the covenant Jesus made with His father.

When we put our faith in Him, we are redeemed from sin, habits, sickness and even death and its sting. We have been lifted up into another realm of life and victory through His power and grace. So when pain comes knocking at your door, or temptation comes knocking at your door, you can confidently and boldly say to it you have no legal right to my life, because of the blood of Jesus, so I bind you and I resist you and you must flee now in Jesus name. The key in this is knowing that you know it has no legal right because of the power of the work of the cross by the Lord Jesus. He has redeemed you from it. When this is a reality it doesn't matter how long it takes for your breakthrough to manifest, to you it is already finished. It is already done.

Ephesians 2:4-6 Because of His great love with which He loved us…He raised us up together and made us sit together in heavenly places in Christ Jesus…

We have been resurrected out of sin and its effects unto a life of total life, total healing, total wholeness, nothing lacking, nothing missing, nothing broken, all because of the power of the work of the cross. You belong to the Lord Jesus, He bought you back from satan through His blood and bought you out of slavery, out of sin, out of habits, out of sickness, out of poverty; satan and his evil, and his evil spirits no longer have any right or access to your life all because of the blood of Jesus.

The Word of God tells us that the blood of Jesus is our covering, and even when we sin that blood still covers your sin and that rebuffs some of the teaching we have had that when you sin it opens the door to evil spirits. If that's the case, that would be happening all day long because we do sin. But, praise be to the Lord Jesus, the blood of Jesus is over us once and for all. Even when you sin, that blood keeps us protected. Now if you go and are not repentant and you get caught up in sin willingly, then you become fair game to the enemy because you choose his lifestyle.

We must have a revelation of this reality that satan has no legal right to our life because Jesus bought us with His blood and He dwells in us, not sin, not darkness, but Jesus through His spirit, we are His temple. In a later chapter we will go into a full teaching that you are the temple where Christ dwells.

Once we see this, our days of oppression, condemnation, weakness and bondage are over. We belong to Jesus. He is your Lord and savior, He is your master, who you lovingly, willingly serve and His blood has redeemed you from satan. You are sitting together with Christ in a place of total victory. It's time to shout a shout of praise to Jesus for this, hallelujah Praise the Lord!

We need to learn to face the enemy and boldly say to him, your sin, your pain, your fear; your poverty cannot stay in my life. I am the redeemed of the Lord and I say so. I am redeemed by the blood of Jesus and all your darkness and bondage has to go now in Jesus name. We must realize as we see ourselves already saved, healed, delivered when Jesus was crucified we then were justified, and we can have a life just as if there never was any sin. Life on earth would be like heaven if Adam never sinned and that's what Jesus came to give us. If Adam never sinned there would be no hate, no rebellion, no curses, no sickness, no fear, etc. That's the life Jesus came to give us through the power of the work of the cross.

It may take some time to take some infirmities to totally leave physically, but from your standpoint you are to face them right now as if it's done in Jesus name.

I was healed when Jesus was crucified, I was justified the very second Jesus was whipped, tortured and murdered. This has to be a reality in us and we must stand upon this truth even if satan tries to put some evil thing upon you, we must know boldly no you don't, you have no legal right to me or my life all because of the blood of Jesus. I am redeemed from this evil in Jesus name. Through the blood of Jesus I am victorious, I am joyous, and I am set free. As you begin to praise Him for this, whatever it is you are facing has to bow its knee just like it did every time Jesus healed the sick, casted out devils, they could not remain.

Acts 10:38 How God anointed Jesus of Nazareth with the Holy Spirit and power who went about doing good who were oppressed of the devil.

I John 3:8 The Son of man was manifested to destroy all the works of the devil.

Just as Jesus did this when He walked the earth, His name through faith in His name will do the same thing today. That is why it has to bow its knee to the Lord Jesus. (see Philippians 2:9-11)

So as we end this chapter, remember this truth. As Jesus was crucified you were declared not guilty and whatever sentence (curses) that were upon or your family because of sin, no longer had a legal right to stay there. Jesus broke that curse on the cross. He redeemed you from it, he forgave you and your family for it setting you free, giving you a new life, His life and as you have put your faith in Him you are redeemed through the power of the work of the cross, every curse of the law, every generational curse was nailed to the cross and as you take your position of faith I am set free through the blood of Jesus and these curses can no longer affect me or my family because we are redeemed, we are no longer sinners, we are saved by grace through faith. We are a new creation, we are victorious, we are not cursed, we are not poor, we are not a failure, and we are redeemed from that.

So begin to expect to be blessed with His joyous fulfilling life. You do not have to continue having the life you have had up to this moment. He has a new redeemed life for you. A life of peace, nothing missing, nothing broken in Jesus name. A life of no bondage, no pain, no death in Jesus name. You may be a believer, but you are not experiencing this. It may be because you are looking for God to do something when in fact He has already done it, and all you need to do is begin to receive that you already have it.

For the power of the work of the cross to have its full effect in our lives, we must truly believe in it and that it's redemption power is greater than the sin or the infirmities we may face and that it's power (the power of the cross) will 24/7, 365 days a year give us the victory and nothing formed against us will ever succeed.

It may look like it's succeeding right now, but in the end it will have to go and it will bow its knee to the Lord Jesus. Be confident in the power of the work of the cross and boldly believe in it, stand upon it in faith even in your darkest hour for you will come into the light of total victory in Jesus name. Your victory will manifest. It has to, it has no options. Jesus guaranteed it when He died on the cross for you and me in Jesus name.

Chapter 3

Your are Qualified

Ephesians 1:7 in Him we have redemption through his blood…

Ephesians 1:11 in Him we also have obtained an inheritance…

Colossians 1:12 giving thanks to our Father who has qualified us to be partakers of the inheritance of the saints in light…

Notice this is something that was done in the past tense, it's not something that is dependent upon anything we do, and it has already been done. The word qualify means to enable, to make able, to make worthy.

Yes it is true Jesus through what he did on the cross has made you worthy of everything that Jesus came to give us as an inheritance, it's yours, and it's a done deal.

The word partakers mean an assigned part, a portion, a share.

Through the blood of Jesus and his work on the cross, He has qualified you for all that is in His kingdom and all the Father gave Him as an inheritance. Nothing you can do can qualify you for ministry, salvation, healing, prosperity, or any other promise He promised in the Word of God. He did all that was required for us to receive His zoe abundant life. He qualified you, He made you able to receive them, He made you worthy of them, He did this and it's a free gift to those who will receive Him as Savior and Lord. As you put your faith in Him and in all He did for you on the cross, as revelation comes to you that it is already done, you then will access it and it will all manifest in your life.

He qualified you for every gift of the Spirit. He qualified you for ministry. He qualified you to reach souls, heal the sick, cast out demons, raise the dead, or do any of the miracles Jesus did.

He qualified you for all these Graces! He qualified you, not your education or the lack thereof can disqualify you. There is nothing you did to qualify you and there is nothing that will disqualify you. He has qualified you to do and to be all He is and all He was when He lived on earth. He has anointed you and He knows all your weaknesses and areas of sin, and yet He still has anointed you and called you. It is not about us, but it is all about His great redemption and grace!!!!!!!!!!!!!!

Do not let man or religious spirits try to deceive you by telling you that you are not qualified, because you had a dark past, or because you have little education, or because you have not had the experience they had, etc. It's his blood and Jesus himself who has qualified you and called you into His kingdom. He knows you, and yet He still has said to you come and we will reach the world together.

So stop trying to qualify yourself, stop feeling less than anyone else, stop trying to figure out what you must do in order to grow, succeed in ministry, or to reach souls. He has fulfilled all the requirements needed; it's through His power and His grace not through anything we could ever do.

We have to get this revelation that it is a done deal, it is finished. This all took place as He died on the cross for you and me, Praise the Lord!!!! You are qualified!!!!!!!!!!!!!!!!!!!!!!!!!!!!!

Chapter 4

You are God's Temple

II Corinthians 6:16 We are the temple of the living God.

II Corinthians 3:16 Do you not know that you are the temple of God and that the Spirit of God dwells in you.

The Word of God says by the Power of the work of the cross, and through the blood of Jesus, and by our receiving Him as Lord, we became by the transforming power of the Holy Spirit, the temple where Jesus, Jehovah, the creator of all things lives and dwells and because of this, sin, sickness and disease, fear and poverty, demons and evil cannot remain. Where He is there is no evil. Think of heaven, God's throne. There is no death, demons, sin, sickness, hate, or evil. Heaven is God's temple as well and in His temple on earth, this same thing is true.

Satan may try to invade God's temple and that's where I John 4:4 comes in.

"Greater is He that is in you than He that is in the world."

Your life, my life, every born again child of God is to live their life on earth just as if Adam and our families never sinned, and if sin never entered, then our life would be like the Garden of Eden, full of peace and fellowship with Jehovah. But, we all know that sin did enter and praise the Lord, Jesus came and got us redeemed back to Jehovah's original plan, and that is John 10:10, to have and enjoy life just as if we never sinned. Remember Romans 5:18 therefore, as one man's offense judgment came to all men resulting in condemnation, even so through one man's righteous act the free gift came to all men resulting in justification of life.

Jesus declared we are not guilty. Sin and all that sin brought into the earth no longer has a legal right to remain in us unless we give it place.

James 4:7 Submit yourself to God, resist the devil and he will flee.

Ephesians 4:27 Give no place to the devil.

Because Jesus lives within us, all that sin brought into the world cannot remain in us. It may try to hold on to your body or your mind, but it cannot, because greater is He that is in us and He will see to it that you are fully redeemed and whole as you stay in faith focused on the power of the work of the cross and how exalted Jesus is. Everything has to bow to Him.

We need to boldly declare that we are God's temple and this sin (name it), the sickness (name it), this lack, cannot remain in this temple. This temple belongs to Jesus. He is my Lord and He dwells in me, and He will not dwell with darkness. The darkness, the oppression, the infirmity will have to bow in Jesus name. Decree it, declare it bowing and then praise Him for it. In His temple dwells Himself, His power and His glory.

In Acts 5:15-16 that at least the shadow of Peter passing by might fall on them...and they were all healed.

How could that be? That sounds like Jesus. It could be because He dwelt within Peter. He Himself is in us. All His power and glory is within us, and is available to flow out of us at any time to save, heal, deliver, and resurrect anyone who taps into Jesus by faith and draws His power and glory out of His temple.

Colossians 1:27 Christ in me the hope of glory.

Because He is in me, I have an expectation to experience all He is and all His glory. No more trying to get it, we already have it. He is in us. All His power is in us. Whatever realm of life you are in, and you need great Holy Spirit power, don't look to get it, don't seek it like it's somewhere else, you already have it. It's inside of you as long as you are born again and filled with His spirit. Just step into it, tap into it, activate it with your faith and words of faith as you declare who you are in Christ, and release His great power and glory into the circumstances and expect it to bow. Watch it bow to the Lord Jesus.

All of this is possible, because He went to the cross and took our sin and He took the sin that came into the world because of Adam's rebellion. He became cursed so we could become blessed. Just as if we never sinned, we can walk with Him just as if we were in heaven with Him physically.

I don't know if while we are on earth, we will ever grasp fully all He did when He went to the cross and was resurrected. That is why we need a greater revelation of Jesus and the power of the work of the cross. All the power you need is already in you, in Jesus name.

Chapter 5

Satan a Defeated Foe

Colossians 2:14-15 Having disarmed principalities and powers, He made a show of them openly triumphing over Him in it.

John 19:30 It is finished!

I John 3:8 The Son of God was manifested that He might destroy all the works of the devil.

Acts 10:38 How God anointed Jesus of Nazareth with the Holy Spirit and power that went about doing good bringing healing to all those oppressed of the devil.

I Peter 5:8 Describes satan as a roaring lion.

Man has allowed the works of the devil and the enemy himself to continue functioning like always, not knowing he is a defeated foe, and it was Jesus who defeated him, stripped him, paralyzed him, and made him a toothless lion. Even to those who know he is defeated, his attacks can be extremely painful and he will try to wear you down spiritually, but if you continue in the fact and truth that satan is defeated, your pain is defeated because of the work of the cross, his evil working against you cannot remain in your life and the victory of the cross will manifest. When unbelief roars at you, just laugh at it and declare it too is defeated. My healing, my need, my breakthrough is already done. Your sin, your habits, your anger, your rebellion, your sickness, your cancer, your arthritis, your heart disease, your poverty, etc., is all defeated and you have the victory by the blood of Jesus and your faith in that great grace. Satan is a defeated foe, Jesus defeated him and his evil works on the cross.

Isaiah was prophesying about the Messiah and what He would do when He came. He may not have known how he would do it, but he knew it would be done. Isaiah 53:4-5, surely He has born our grief's (sicknesses) carried our sorrows (pain whether emotional or physical). We esteemed Him stricken, smitten by God and afflicted, but He was wounded (pierced through) for our transgressions, He was bruised (crushed) for our iniquities and the chastisement for our peace (shalom, wholeness, completeness, nothing missing, nothing broken) was upon Him and by His stripes we are healed.

Not going to be healed, but we are healed. Isaiah saw the Messiah paying the price for man's total salvation, and that in it, satan, sin, sickness, pain would be defeated. He suffered so we could be whole, sound, and complete and delivered from satan's hold. We must see our salvation as complete, totally done. It's provided for. All we have to do is receive it by faith.

You don't have to fight to get healed or delivered, it's already yours in Jesus name, but you do have to fight to hold onto it, because satan will try to steal it from you.

I had a vision in my spirit of a large hand over a head, and in this vision, I realized that satan was holding God's people in bondage and oppressing them, and just as I saw this hand holding tightly onto a person's head, I saw a sledge hammer come that was swung with a mighty force and hit this hand that was oppressing and holding God's people in bondage, and immediately this hand was crippled, it was totally paralyzed, it was now weak to where it could not hold God's people captive, and that's what Jesus did on the cross of Calvary for you and I.

I declare over you and your life, that any hold that the enemy has had on you, on your family, on your body, in your mind, on your finances, in our nation, that the Lord Jesus is rising up like a mighty man of war and swinging the sledge hammer of His Word and smashing that hold and releasing the captives, in Jesus name, I say that we are set free, I say that those holds will never hold us again in bondage through the blood of Jesus and by the power of the work of the cross, I declare it so in Jesus name.

Chapter 6

Prayer Becomes a Guarantee

Because of the work of the cross, the Lord's Prayer becomes a guarantee.

The first thing to understand concerning the Lord's Prayer is that it's not something we are to ask for, but we are to decree it, declare it from a position it's already been provided for. It is our inheritance and it belongs to us. All because of Jesus, His blood and what He did when He went to the cross for us.

Matthew 6:9-13 Our Father in heaven, hallowed be your name, your Kingdom come, your will be done on earth as it is in heaven. Give us this day our daily bread.

Whatever we need for this day, favor, love, joy, revelation, protection, money, food, health, a sound mind, it is already provided for us according to His riches in glory through the power of the work of the cross, and all we need to do is agree with it, decree it as if it's already done. Rest and trust in Him for His provision. The mistake many make is they pray this from a position of asking God to do something as if it's not done yet, as if they're waiting for something to happen and in doing so we pray in unbelief and may not realize it. When Jesus said, it is finished He meant everything we ever will need has already been provided for us through the work He did on the cross.

Job 22:28 Says decree a thing and it will happen.

Ephesians 1:7 In Him we have redemption through His blood…according to the riches of His grace.

Philippians 4:19 My God will supply all your need according to His riches in glory by Christ Jesus.

These riches in glory that our needs are met by that we can access at any time were provided by the Lord Jesus when He went to the cross. We need revelation that through the power of the work of the cross, we can access the riches that are our inheritance by the grace of God through the Lord Jesus Christ. We must learn how to access them with our faith, and we must be taught by the Holy Spirit on how to get those riches flowing in our lives because they are already provided for by the Lord Jesus.

Back to Matthew 6, forgive us our debts as we forgive our debtors.

Your forgiveness and the ability to forgive is a grace released to us through and because of the cross. You are forgiven because of the work Jesus did on the cross and we can forgive others even when it's difficult, because of the work Jesus did on the cross. We are not asking Him to do something that is not yet done. It is already done.

Lead us not into temptation, but deliver us from the evil one.

We have been delivered from every demonic attack, strategy through the power of the work of the cross, and as we decree this, as we know they are already defeated by the Lord Jesus, as we know we have been given power over them (demons) we know Jesus through His cross has already delivered us from Satan, his demons and every evil attempt to trick us, bind us, lead us astray, afflict us or persecute us. We are the delivered, we are not trying to get delivered, we are delivered. This we need to boldly decree even when it does not look like it. If you have a habit, if there's a sin that has dominated you, that you have not been able to get free of, don't ask God to do something about it, because He's already done all He's going to do. What you need to realize is that you are already delivered and to learn to use your authority in the name of Jesus declaring against that evil spirit that you are delivered from them, they have no right to your life because you belong to Jesus, and you are evicting them and if they continue to harass you, just continue believing you are delivered, praising the Lord Jesus that you are delivered and resist the thoughts of unbelief with what God says and who God says you are. You are the delivered, you are the healed, you are the victorious, all because of what Jesus did on the cross.

Back to Matthew 6 for yours is the Kingdom and the power of the glory forever.

He gets all the praise, all the glory, for all He has provided through the cross. There was more done at the cross than just Jesus dying so we could be forgiven.

All things were provided through this great work of grace. All we need to do is learn how to receive it, trust in it, praise Him for it and walk in it.

Great revelation is being released concerning the power of the work of the cross. The power of the work of the cross will totally free and release us into the blessed life He came to give us in Jesus name. When we truly see this, it will shift us into a more peaceful, fruitful way of living. It will shift us from self, meaning we will stop living like and thinking like what more can we do to get the break through. We will realize He has already done it. So many times, we are trying to get something we already possess. We at times have asked why is it taking so long, and at least in part, you may not have understood that it's already done even if you don't see it manifesting in your life yet.

Everything in life you will ever need has already been given, planned, and prepared for you, whether it's a house, a job, to reach souls, a building to meet in, a car, food, the desires of your heart, a family, etc., so no matter how impossible it may look, He has already met your need according to His riches in glory when He went to the cross on your behalf.

As we receive this revelation we will praise Him more and more. We will shout with the victory even if it looks like we are totally defeated, because we are not going by what we see, we are going by what was done at the cross of Calvary.

Whatever the Lord is telling you to do, build a new building, move across the country, start a media ministry, write books, whatever it is, He has already gone before you and prepared the way and met every need.

Exodus 23:20 Behold I have sent an angel before you to keep you in the way and to bring you to the place which I have prepared.

So no matter what it is Jesus has already provided it for you.

Chapter 7

By Grace Through Faith

Ephesians 2:8-9 By grace are you saved through faith and not of yourselves. It is the gift of God, not of works lest any man boasts.

The Greek word for saved is sozo which means saved, healed, rescued from danger, sound. To save a suffering one from disease, make well, restore to health, to preserve one who is in danger of destruction.

Wow! This is our great salvation! By grace, by what Jesus did on the cross we have been saved, healed, rescued from danger, and rescued from disease or from accidents and every form of evil! It was His gift to us when we put our faith in Him as savior and Lord. It already belongs to us, it's ours through the power of the work of the cross. You are saved and healed right now by his wonderful grace!!!!!!!!!!!!!

How many times have we heard people boasting in the accomplishments of what

Jesus provided for them by saying things like I fasted and I got a miracle or I did this or that and something happened. Without realizing it, they are putting the focus on what they have done and not what He did, there is so much performance works teaching today it's unreal. We do not focus on the work of the cross. We run to seminars on how to have a growing church or how to prosper greater or how to have a better business and all these things are good, but one thing is the focus; it was his grace that blessed you not your works! We must shift our focus on His great work on the cross and on His grace not be focused on our works even though they are biblical.

We must repent of all boasting and pride in Jesus name! We must cover that sin with the blood of Jesus.

I cannot tell you how many times I have prayed what more must I do in order to receive the breakthrough we need. As I did this, my focus was on my performance, my works, instead of what Jesus already provided for me on the cross and that it was already done and all I needed to do was see it as done and walk by faith that it is done and call it done by seeking His wisdom on how to proceed.

John 19:30 says it is finished, not going to be, but it is finished. Your need is met, you now lack for nothing as Jesus provided it all. A family member's salvation, healing, or a job need, or whatever it needed, is already provided for them. As you believe it is done it will manifest for them.

Whatever the need is the grace of God has already provided it!

Remember, it's not about how much you pray, study God's Word, give, fast, etc., even though these things are our lifestyle, it's all about the grace He provided for you on the cross so you can have and enjoy life abundantly!

Ephesians 4:7 says but to each one of us grace was given…

Everyone in the body of Christ has been given grace to receive His anointing and provision of the cross.

Romans 4:17 says calling those things that do not exist as though they did…Being fully persuaded…

The grace of God within you will bring into manifestation what Jesus has already provided for you on the cross, as you call it as done!

We live our life by the faith Jesus lived by (Galatians 2:20). As we were born again, He gave us His grace and His faith to live by, it's not our own. We should never point to anything that we have reduced spiritually as the reason we received. It's all by grace through faith in what He has already provided on the cross for you. When we call those things that be not as though they were, it's not our faith that manifests through them, it's the faith that Jesus lived by that He imparted into us when we were born again. You can read this in Roman's 12:3.

We need to repent of every time we have tried to glorify ourselves because of the answers to prayers and miracles we have been graced with to experience. Father, we apply the blood of Jesus over every time we have exalted ourselves and touched the glory and the praise you deserve in Jesus name. We repent of this. We receive deliverance from the effects of that sin in Jesus name. Every time we have boasted in ourselves, every time we have been in pride we cover that sin with the blood of Jesus, and the effects of that sin we declare are broken off of us in Jesus name. Thank you for forgiving us in Jesus name.

It's all about grace through faith. Whatever your anointing or position in life is, it's not of yourself but all about His grace through faith, and He gets all the praise and the glory in Jesus name.

The people that probably struggle with this type of message are people who went to school and received great training like a physician, surgeon, psychiatrist, or minister, but they must realize it's not about their education, but it's about His grace that grace them to be who they are.

For those who are your everyday people, the grace of God is upon you just as much to do great things for His kingdom. When your heart gives Him all the praise you will see great manifestations in Jesus name.

Chapter 8

When Jesus was Resurrected I Received New Life

Romans 6:4 says therefore, we were buried with Him through baptism into death. Just as Christ was raised from the dead by the glory of the Father, even so we also should walk in newness of life.

Romans 8:11 says if the spirit of Him who raised Jesus from the dead dwells in you, He who raised Christ from the dead will also give life to your mortal bodies through His spirit who dwells in you.

John 10:10 I came to give you life and that life more abundantly.

Before Jesus could be raised from the dead to a glorified life, a zoe God kind of life far above all pain and evil; He had to suffer and die. When we are water baptized into Him, we too die a death of an old way of life which lived to sin, loved to sin. When we accept His work on the cross, when He was resurrected we too were raised up into the kind of abundant life Jesus lived in, walks in even right now as the glorified exalted Son of God, far above all sin, pain and evil. His grace and power lifts us up into a heavenly realm, an empowerment to live on earth as He is in heaven.

I John 4:17 says as He is, so are we in this world.

Think about it, as Jesus is right now, He is pain free, He has no cancer, He has no allergies, He has no heart disease, He has no poverty, He has no strife or any other thing that the world experiences. When He was raised from the dead we were raised up to the same position that He is in, all because and all through His gift of grace and the power of the work of the cross we have been resurrected into this new life. This life is supernatural and those outside of Christ can never experience it.

We do not have to continue the life of living in pain, in sin, in oppression or limitations. We have been raised up to sit together with Him in heavenly places.

Ephesians 2:6 Raised us up together and made us sit together in heavenly places in Christ Jesus.

He has resurrected us out of the life of death unto a life far above sin, pain, demons, curses, etc. We have His life dwelling in us.

WOW! Praise the Lord! You are resurrected not going to be, just reach out with your faith and grab hold of this grace, this new resurrected life in Jesus name. He came, suffered and died to give it to us. He made us worthy to receive it. It's His grace coming towards us like a hurricane to give you an exalted; glorious far above all you can think or ask type of life. It's what the resurrection is all about.

It is my belief few of God's people have yet to tap into this kind of life in its fullness, but it's available to us by His finished works on the cross. By grace through faith it's yours, just receive it and accept it as a done deal. It's your inheritance from Him. Just as if you found out a rich relative left you $30 million dollars, for you to receive it, all you have to do is accept this check.

It's more than words can express. It's supernatural, it's heavenly. It's what it means in part that we are to live life in the Spirit so just take it.

If its sin you have been resurrected out of it, if its pain, infirmity, fears, poverty, etc., you have been resurrected out of it. Praise you Jesus.

As you receive this revelation and insight, your love for Him and your worship of Him will greatly increase and your dependence upon your works, your performance will die off and you will see that there is nothing you can do to get this type of life from God. It's all been given to us by His grace through our faith in His son and He gets all the praise and all the glory.

In Philippians 3:10 Paul prayed that I would know Him and the power of His resurrection. Paul had an insight that there was more to this resurrection life and resurrection power than the church was currently living, and we too have to realize this. There is so much more and we need to press in to it, because it is our inheritance and the thief will try to stop you from it, but as you hold on to the Word of God, and as you believe it is finished, it will break through and it will manifest. You may have a war on your hands for a season, but persevere, the victory is yours! Accept it, believe, and stand on it. As He is, so are we in this world.

Chapter 9

Stand and Trust

What do you do when symptoms persist when they seem like they are not budging when the pain is still there, when the lack is still there, when the problem is still there. Here are two words that I am hearing. Stand and trust! As I am writing this I have been dealing with blood pressure issues and allergies that affect my inner ear that cause light headedness. I live in an area where this abounds; so I have to live on the truth that I received from the Lord, and that is by His stripes I am healed. My deliverance is finished!

When we know we are redeemed from heart disease, allergies, etc., and we know that all that our body needs has already been provided for us on the cross, and yet there are still symptoms, we must continue standing on the word of truth, the Word of God, and standing on the God of the Word and trust it will come to pass because He said so. For this to happen we need a greater grace, a greater boldness, a greater strength, a greater revelation of simply trusting in Him. How we receive this at least in part, is to just soak in His presence. Put on some anointing healing worship CD's and soak in His glory. Let His Word and His Spirit saturate your spirit, soul and body. Go over the scriptures that you have received from Him concerning your situation and decree them as if it is done and praise Him for who He is. You may need to do this for months and maybe even for years, but according to God's Word it has to come to pass, He guaranteed it.

It may not be an easy thing to do, but that's why we walk by faith and not by sight.

Jeremiah 3:16 It shall come to pass when you are multiplied and increased.

Isaiah 65:4 It shall come to pass that before they call I will answer.

Mark 11:23 Those things He says will come to pass.

Acts 2:21 It shall come to pass that whosoever shall call upon the name of the Lord shall be saved (remember our teaching that saved means healed, delivered, rescued out of disease).

Romans 5:2 By whom also we have access by faith into His grace wherein we stand and rejoice in the hope of the glory of God.

John 11:44 Jesus showed us the glory of God when Lazarus was resurrected from the dead so we can stand by faith expecting His glory to resurrect us out of whatever infirmity or sin you may be dealing with.

Romans 11:20 Thou standest by faith.

So in order to stand on the fact we are already whole by the power of the work of the cross, we must take a stand on that fact and never budge, never question it, and when the thoughts come to you and they will come, how come it's taking so long, you just keep declaring by faith that your mountain is moving and your healing miracle is already done no matter what you see. If need be, keep taking the medicine, keep using whatever advantage that God has graced our world with in order to receive a better quality of life, but don't get dependent on the natural but stay focused on the spiritual.

Psalm 22:8 He trusted in the Lord that He would deliver him.

Psalm 28:7 The Lord is my strength and my shield, my heart trusts in Him.

Psalm 37:40 the Lord shall help them and deliver them. He shall deliver them from the wicked and save them because they trust in Him.

David wrote these psalms when he was going through very difficult times in his life. He received revelation concerning standing and trusting in the Lord. We have to stand and trust in the finished works of Jesus not in our performance. It is those who trust in Him that receive from Him. We have to learn to trust that His Word is at work in us even when we don't see it or feel it. We need to declare that we believe God's word and its power is at work in our bodies, minds, families, finances, ministry, and nation. We must continue doing this and keep doing as a lifestyle, as a way of life, even when the miracle manifests continue standing, continue believing that it is finished in Jesus name.

Chapter 10

A Full Supply

When Jesus became poor you became fully supplied in every area of your life no matter the economy, or how high the cost of living is!!!!!!!!!!!!!!!!!!!!

2 Corinthians 8:9 For you know the grace of our Lord Jesus Christ that though He was rich yet for your sakes He became poor that you through His poverty might become rich.

Grace means unearned favor.

Rich means fully, completely in every way, supplied.

Poverty means not enough, lacking, struggling.

The first thing that stands out to me is that this is a work of grace by the Lord Jesus and not something we can earn by our good works, education, etc.

It is a free gift from our Lord Jesus Christ when we received him as savior. The great wealth of heaven He left behind when He was born of a virgin and came to this earth became yours by grace through faith. This wealth consists of spiritual, financial, and material things. It is ours by inheritance and not by our works. Through this inheritance you have a full supply.

John 10:10 Jesus came to give you life and that life more abundantly.

One version says He came to give you life to enjoy. We will not enjoy life if we are bound by lack! Jesus wants you to enjoy life and the things He had created for your enjoyment!

II Corinthians 9:8 God is able to make all grace abound to you, that you always having all sufficiency in all things…

Part of the power of the work of the cross is to impart into you the grace to have a full supply so you and your family will enjoy life!!!!!!!!!!!!!!!!!!!

Have you ever noticed that in Paul's writings he uses the phrase "according to his riches in glory"? This describes the exalted life we are to have when we are in Christ. We are not to struggle, but we are to have a full supply. Jesus provided it for us through the power of the work of the cross and it's up to you to accept it as truth or reject it and go without.

Romans 9:23 He might make known to you the riches of His glory on the vessels of mercy (that's you and me) ...which He prepared ...

Jesus prepared for you in Glory a full supply in every realm of life. He did this before He came to the earth and it's up to us to accept them or reject them by how we believe. If we see this in our redemption and mix our faith with it and say yes amen, then it will begin to manifest. But if we disagree with it because our minds have not rightly divided God's Word, then we will struggle. That does not mean you will not have to battle for what is yours in Chris, but it does mean it legally belongs to you and if you stay in faith breakthrough will come. Always remember it took Abraham 25 years before his inheritance manifested.

Philippians 4:19 My God will supply all your need according to His riches in Glory by Christ Jesus.

Ephesians 1:18 The eyes of your understanding being enlightened that you may know what are the riches of His glory of His inheritance in the saints.

Part of your inheritance is riches or a full supply from heaven.

Here Paul was praying the churches eyes would be opened to see and understand just what is theirs in Christ so they are not robbed of it through unbelief or ignorance (not knowing).

Here are some other scriptures that mention " His riches in Glory".

Ephesians 2:7

Ephesians 3:8, 20

Ephesians 3:16
Colossians 1:27

To me this says it's God's will that everything He does is through His riches in glory by His son Jesus, not according to my job or lack thereof. So be encouraged in this area that you already have His grace to provide you a full supply. It is already yours. You do not have to try to get it, it's your inheritance. Jesus provided it for you on the cross just like he provided forgiveness, but it did not affect your life until you found out about it and accepted it as a done deal. So accept a full supply as a done deal and begin to praise Him for the fullness of the power of the work of the cross.

Chapter 11

When Jesus Was Rejected I Was Grafted In

Isaiah 53:3 (Isaiah prophesying about what the Messiah would go through on our behalf). He is despised and rejected by men, a man of sorrows acquainted with grief.

The bible and God's covenant people were written to the Jews; it was the Jews who rejected Him (not all of them, mostly just the religious leaders), and it was their rejection that was prophesied as well as the pain that would come to our life when people reject us. It was because of the Jews rejecting Jesus as Messiah that the gentiles were grafted in. All the promises in the old covenant were to Abraham and his seed (Jesus Christ).

As a matter of fact, the whole bible was written by the Jews to Jewish people until Jesus came and reached the gentiles as well. Think about this, all of God's promises were to the Jews and if Jesus did not come we could never have been saved or blessed with God's blessings, so I am very grateful to Jesus for His great sacrifice so I can be saved!!!!!!!!!!!! It now belongs to all those who are now new creations in Christ Jesus (II Corinthians 5:17) not whether we have been born Jewish, Praise the Lord.

John 3:16 Who ever believes in Him should not perish but have everlasting life.

John 3: 17 That the world through Him might be saved.

So when we believe in Him, all God's promises of total salvation belongs to us by inheritance. Never forget Jesus is a Jew and we are adopted into His Jewish family.

Galatians 3:14 That the blessing might come upon the gentiles in Christ Jesus that we might receive the promise of the Spirit through faith.

So all the promises to the Jew and new creation become our inheritance.

Romans 11:11-23 Salvation has come to the gentiles…Riches for the gentiles… were grafted in among them… Branches were broken off that we might be grafted in.

So this reveals to me that Jesus on the cross when He was rejected by His own people grafted me in into His family and Kingdom through the new creation process which is a work of the Holy Spirit, and I am now a grafted in spiritual Jew by spiritual birth in Christ Jesus.

Galatians 3:2 If you be Christ's then are you Abraham's seed and heirs according to the promise.

Galatians 4:4-7 Because you are sons, God has sent forth, the Spirit of His son into your hearts crying Abba Father, therefore you are no longer a slave but a son and if a son then an heir of God through Christ.

Wow! Awesome! Praise the Lord!!!!!!!!!!!!!!!!!! We are the sons of the living God, no longer forsaken but loved, wanted and accepted. When you are adopted you are highly chosen. In a natural birth you cannot pick and choose your children, but with God He specifically chose you even knowing you would sin He still chose you. That is an awesome love and it is all because of Jesus and the work He did on the cross for you and me. All that is Christ's is now yours through inheritance.

Romans 8:16 You are a joint heir with Christ.

Never doubt you are accepted, loved all because of Jesus and his work on the cross. You can't earn it, work for it, it is a gift to you when you believe in Jesus and His finished works of the cross. It's yours by grace through faith.

Chapter 12

Fullness of Life

Colossians 2:10 You too have everything when you are in Him.

Through the power of the work of the cross which is the finished works of Jesus, we have the fullness of life in Jesus name!

John 10:10 I have come to give your life and that life more abundantly.

Jesus did not come to give you a great marriage and then have you suffer, say in your body. He did not come to give you great wealth and then suffer in your marriage or family or ministry, etc. He came to give us the same life He has right now at the Fathers right hand.

1 John 4:17 As He is now so are we in this world.

Psalm 23:1 The Lord (Jesus) is my Shepherd and I shall not want (or lack).
John 5:21 The Son gives life.

John 11:25 I am the resurrection and the life.

Romans 4:17 God who gives life.

This is the reality and revelation of the new covenant, no more curses or punishment to the believer only life and that life more abundantly. This also is what it means to be under grace and not the law, which ministered death and judgment if you did not keep every ordinance of God. Praise God we are delivered into His Kingdom of grace and life all through the power of the work of the cross by Jesus Christ.

2 Peter 1:2-3 Grace and peace be multiplied to you in the knowledge of God and of Jesus our Lord, as His divine power has given us all things that pertain to life and godliness through the knowledge of Him.

His grace and shalom (wholeness, completeness, nothing missing, nothing broken) is being multiplied to us in the kingdom of what Jesus has already provided for us through the cross and resurrection which has given us the fullness of life in Christ Jesus in every area of life and godliness. He does not want us to be lacking in any area of life. He already provided it all, all we have to do is say yes Lord so be it!

Say it out loud. I have, not going to get, fullness of life in Jesus name through the power of the work of the cross and resurrection in Jesus name! I have no lack only abundance of life in Christ Jesus! Declare this every day as often as possible so your mind becomes renewed to this fact, and so you never accept this world's limitations in Jesus name! Be specific, if your back hurts say it to your back, if you lack financially say it to your finances, if you lack success in ministry say it to your ministry and expect God's great grace to manifest in you, upon you, and through you in Jesus name!!!!!!!!!!!!!!!!!!!!!!!!!!

Romans 8:11 The same Spirit who raised Jesus from the dead dwells in you and will also give you life.

Acts 10:38 Reveals that Jesus went about giving life through healing all those oppressed of the devil.

If you don't have fullness of life in some area of your life, you have an oppression of the enemy which he tries to put on every one, so don't be discouraged, don't condemn yourself just receive His grace in giving you life in abundance. Don't try to spiritually earn it, don't work for it just accept it and access it by believing it's yours and it's a done deal in Jesus name! We all have been there and most of us are still learning and growing in this great grace.

Think about how He is every part of His being, His life is full of life, and this is what is available to us through His grace when we believe Him and His finished works He did on the cross for us. This is the kind of life He has provided for us who name Him as Lord, Savior, Messiah. We need to stop accepting anything less than fullness of life.

No matter what area of your life that you have little in, His plan is for you to have His abundance of life in that area. Know this, whatever the lack it is not of Him. In many cases it's because we accept the world's limitations as final word instead of accepting God's unlimited provision as the final word. How you do that is to continue to stand and that you have His full life no matter what all because he says so!

Chapter 13

Righteousness Through His Grace

Romans 3:22 The righteousness of God which is the faith of Jesus Christ unto all and upon all that believe...

Romans 3:24-26 Be justified freely by His grace through the redemption that is in Jesus Christ... Whom God has set forth to be propitiation through faith in His blood to declare His righteousness for the remission of sins... To declare at this time His righteousness.

Romans 4:5 To him that worketh not but believeth on him that justified the ungodly His faith is counted as righteous.

Romans 5:17-19 The gift of grace and the gift of righteousness... even so by righteousness of one, the free gift came upon all men unto justification of life... so that by the obedience of one shall many be saved.

Romans 5:21 Even so might grace reign through righteousness unto eternal life by Jesus Christ our Lord.

Romans 10:10 For with the heart man believes unto righteousness and with the mouth confession is made unto salvation…

II Corinthians 5:21 He who knew no sin became sin so that we might become the righteousness of God in Christ.

Through the power of the work of the cross the grace of our Lord Jesus has made us in right standing with God just as if we never sinned. This took place the moment we put our faith in the finished works of Jesus for our total salvation and blessing, we at that moment received his righteousness or we became who Jesus is and was as He ministered on this earth, Gods child. We were graced with all His gifts, character, provision and love that the Father bestowed upon Jesus. We became anointed, full of power to live like He lived, to do all the miracles He did, to reach souls in multitude fashions like He did etc.

It's all because of what Jesus did on the cross for us. Sin entered, death entered, sickness entered, poverty entered, evil entered because of what Adam and Eve did. Just like salvation, righteousness, eternal life, healing, prosperity, preservation entered into us through one, Jesus Christ. As you believe in Him, accept His finished work on the cross you are newly created into Christ, into being Him, becoming just like Him, an exact recreation of Himself on earth to live like He lived and to help others, minister to others just like He did with supernatural power and grace, not to condemn, not to make them religious, not to make them live by the law, but to help them, forgive them, heal them, transform them out of darkness into His great Kingdom, to resurrect them to where sin, the curse has no effect over them all because of what He did, not because of anything we ever did, His great grace has recreated us into Himself praise the Lord.

Stop thinking like earthly carnal man and think like a new creation newly created into His right standing with God. You are a supernatural Holy Spirit empowered person who can do all things through Christ!!!!!!!!!!!!!! Just like Jesus did, we are one with Him, we need to see this and comprehend this. We are in Him and He is in us we are one. Wow… all by His grace coming to us through the power of the work of the cross! On the day we were born again we became him on the earth, his voice, just like he was the Fathers voice, just like he and the Father were one, we are one with Christ, this is amazing! That's why we can do all he did and greater things.

II Corinthians 5:17 Therefore if any man is in Christ, he is a new creation old things have passed away and all things have become new.

When we are born again something happens within us. Everything that is of sin dies and we not only are forgiven and changed from the inside out, but greater than that, we become like Him, we become Him to a lost world. We can do all He did; reach souls, cast our demons, raise the dead, bring joy to the oppressed, walk on water, turn water into wine, etc.

What that means is whatever problem we face in our own lives or in ministering to others, it must obey, it must bow to the name of Jesus. We can face it fearlessly! He is in us, we are in Him, and we abide in Him so it's actually Jesus through us healing, raising, and blessing not us. It's His grace flowing through us as we are just yielded vessels. There is nothing you can do to earn this just yield to Him let his power and grace flow through you in Jesus name!

Have you ever thought about how new Spirit filled believers flow in the gifts? One of the reasons is because they do nothing but through His grace, they don't try to qualify by works of prayer, fasting, giving they just step out and flow. They are not yet brainwashed with a bunch of laws, restrictions of man. They are not depending on their own spirituality and works to minister, know nothing but speak what the Spirit says and do what Jesus did; lay hands on the sick, prophesy, rebuke demons, etc. They have not gotten entangled in what are Christian religious laws that bind you not liberate you. We need to get back to the place of grace and power just yielding to the Spirit and doing the works of Jesus.

When we realize that we are righteous by grace through faith and that we are one with Him, we are Him, He is in us we will know nothing is impossible to us all because of His great grace and the finished works on Calvary, we are a new creation in right standing with God as if we never sinned, totally justified, qualified and anointed empowered for ministry. This is awesome to think, everywhere 24/7, 365 days a year, Jesus is where I am and his grace is ready to flow out of us to a hurting world. We are not God, we are just where He chose to abide and because of that nothing is impossible to the believer.

Ephesians 2:7 We are seated together with Him in heavenly places.

He has lifted us up into a realm of total grace and power far above all principalities and powers just as He is above them and they have to bow to Him. He graced us with that same grace and power and as we represent Him on earth. He saves, heals, delivers, blesses through us because He is in us, never forget that!

He has made you righteous, He has filled you with His righteousness, the emphasis is on His righteousness, in Him, through Him God looks on us as if we never sinned, praise the Lord!!!!!!!!!!!!

Chapter 14

Jesus Took Every Infirmity

Through the finished works of the cross Jesus took into His body every infirmity, every weakness of your soul, He left nothing to chance, it is finished. He took it so you could take into your life divine health which includes wholeness, soundness in your mind.

Galatians 3:13 Christ has redeemed us from the curse of the law so that the blessing of Abraham might come upon the gentiles…

Think of millions of people as the children of Israel left Egypt, the bible says there was not one feeble among them; that is divine health through the grace of God.

Psalm 105:37 There was not one feeble person among their tribes.

Matthew 8:16-17 He cast out spirits with His Word and healed all that were sick that it might be fulfilled which was spoken by the prophet Isaiah, Himself took our infirmities and bare our sickness.

Infirmity means physical weakness and moral weakness.

Every infirmity we may have, every weakness we may have in our bodies, minds, emotions, finances, etc., He took upon himself so we could be healed. He became that sin nature so we could be whole, sound and complete. This, Jesus did when He went to the cross on our behalf. Every infirmity means every single one of them; no matter how small or how big, it is finished He took them for you. He exchanged His health for our infirmities, praise the Lord.

Luke 13:11-16 Jesus said ought not this daughter of Abraham be loosed whom satan had bound?

First notice that satan was the cause of her infirmity; he is the cause of your infirmity as well. Second, He healed her of her infirmity and if Jesus did this for a daughter of Abraham, then He will do it for all the children of Abraham, He will manifest what He provided on the cross for you. This is in part the blessing of Abraham that is ours because of Jesus, it is finished, it belongs to you!

We must get the revelation that every single infirmity He took, He became_____ so we could be healed and not feeble. We must never accept any infirmity as part of who we are.

I would suggest to make a list of every infirmity you face and battle and then declare to every single one of them that Jesus took you, He removed you from my life, you have no legal right to my life all because of the power of the work of the cross and God's power full grace that heals me with the stripes of Jesus.

Remember Jesus said in Mark 11:23 to speak to the mountain to be removed and it would obey. He did not say to rehearse the curse and talk how bad it is, He said speak to it. As you speak you are not hoping it will be removed and you will be healed, KNOW you are speaking to it from a position that it is already finished, it's a done deal and you are just releasing your faith in the fact it is finished and it cannot stay in you and no matter how long it takes to manifest you will not change your belief and confession all because of what Jesus did on the cross.

Just as Peter saw in 1 Peter 2:24 that by His stripes He was healed looking back at the cross, we must do the same and receive the revelation looking back at the cross that we too are healed of every single infirmity, not going to be healed but we are healed by the blood that flowed from Jesus as they beat Him, not because we do not feel it or see it no longer. Holy Spirit open our eyes to this fact in Jesus name!

When this happens in you, Praise will explode out of you towards the Lord Jesus giving Him thanks and glory for the work He did on the cross for you.

Luke 5:21 But so much more went there a fame abroad of Him and great multitudes came together to hear and be healed of their infirmities.

Luke 7:21 He cured many of their infirmities…

Romans 8:26 Likewise the Holy Spirit helps my infirmities…
As we pray in tongues the Holy Spirit goes to work healing you and causing you to overcome every infirmity through the grace that comes to us through the power of the

work of the cross! He delivers you into wholeness, completeness so you lack for nothing, He delivers you into a sound healthy mind and thought life as well, The Holy Spirit does everything Jesus provided for us on the cross.

The revelation of this chapter is that He wants you healed of every infirmity and that is already done and by His grace if you will just accept it, the power of God will breakthrough in you with your miracle. Just enter His rest that it is finished and by His grace you believe to receive it and then rejoice!

Acts 1:8 Says we have been given the power of the Holy Spirit so that we can enforce the power and grace that Jesus provided on the cross and be a witness of that great salvation, not just for ourselves but for the whole world. As we meet the sick, demonized, poor, hurting we can release the grace He gave to us through the power of the work of the cross when we believed in Him and were Spirit filled, and set them free in Jesus name! Not asking Him to do it, because He already did it, but by enforcing the power of what He already did on Calvary for all men!!!!!!

So we declare that we, our families, our bodies, our finances, our children are healed of every infirmity! We declare these things in Jesus name according to Job 22:28 declare a thing and it will come to pass!!!!!!!!!!!!!!!!!!! Thank you Jesus!!!!!!!!!!!!!!!!!!!

Chapter 15

Unbelief

Our problem is not with believing that God can or even will do something, our challenge is according to the new covenant is to believe it is already done, or I have it even though I do not see it yet, that is called unbelief.

Romans 12:3 We have been given the measure of faith…. Not a measure we all have within us the same measure Jesus lived by.

When we were born again the faith of the son of God was deposited inside of us, (see Galatians 2:20). We have the very same faith Jesus lived by, ministered through, trusted His Father with, raised the dead through, performed miracles through, never doubted His Father with. The very same faith He turned water into wine with, walked on water with. So our problem is not faith, but it is fear, doubt and unbelief.

Mark 9:14-29 Reveals to us that the disciples could not do something that Jesus empowered them and told them to do, and that was heal and deliver people from demons (Matthew 10:1). And Jesus said it was because of their unbelief.

Mark 6:5-6 Jesus could not do any miracles except He healed a few with minor ailments. Why? Because of their unbelief.

Unbelief basically ether refuses to believe something is true or according to the new covenant does not believe it is finished, or it is already done through God's grace through the finished works of the cross, or as I like to say, through the power of the work of the cross. We ask for God to do something, heal, provide or save, when he said, you lay hands on the sick and they will be healed.

Nowhere does it ever say to ask God to heal, cast out a demon, or raise the dead or to save a lost person, it says for you to do something and basically God's grace and power will flow through you to heal, save, raise, etc. Even in ministering salvation to the lost according to Romans 10:8-10, it says to accept or agree with, that Jesus is Lord and to believe He was raised from the dead by the power of God and you will receive salvation, nowhere does it say to pray and ask God to save the lost, if we do pray that way we are in unbelief.

Now God can ignore our unbelief and extend his mercy and do it anyways, but it still does not change the fact we are praying in unbelief if we ask God to do something He told you to do and that He empowered you with his grace and power to do it. The devil is very deceptive and he will keep us bound to unbelief if we do not see that we are praying in unbelief and not in faith.

The devil will also deceive us into asking God for something that God says is already ours and he will attack our thoughts and try to get us in unbelief by saying if it is already done how come its taking so long for you to get it or where is it or you look at how you feel or what your senses are saying to you. It is at these moments if you receive those thoughts and speak them out loud he has deceived you into unbelief and it's not that your faith is not working, but you have yielded to unbelief making your faith and the finished works of Jesus void of power to do you any good. What we need to do is when those thoughts of unbelief attack you is not to accept them by saying what Jesus said in John 19: 30 it is finished. I don't care how long it takes I believe my healing, deliverance or whatever else I need is already done, its mine in Jesus name and just begin to praise Him with all your might.

We must recognize when unbelief comes and is at work against you. We must never accept it but resist it by standing on the finished works of the cross in Jesus name. The devil might say to you, you will never receive that miracle and your response is that is correct because it is already done, I don't need to get it, I already have it in Jesus name and then just rejoice in Jesus! Even if it takes a lifetime we must believe it is already done. That is true spiritual warfare!

Remember if the care of something worries you, then that tells you unbelief is at work. If you are anxious about a promise from God, that too tells us unbelief is at work and you stepped out of believing that it is finished.

1 Peter 5:7 Cast all your cares upon Him for He cares for you.

Unbelief has robbed us of God's best, but God's grace is greater and as we grow in grace and in the knowledge of the finished works of the cross we will be avenged of all the enemy stole and deceived from us in Jesus name! So let's rise up and say whatever it is we need it is finished and there is no, none, zero condemnation in Christ Jesus!!!!!!!!!!!!!!!!!!

Chapter 16

Enter His Rest

Religion and religious deception tries to put the answer on self. For example, we need to pray more, give more in order to get a breakthrough in some area of life. According to the new covenant it's already finished. It's not dependent upon what we do, but its dependent upon what has already been done on the cross. Everything we do spiritually is out of love for the Kingdom and to help others not to get answers, because it is finished.

Stop working and just enter the rest of living by grace and faith in the finished works of Jesus. Relax, do not be so anxious, and enjoy living.

Hebrews 4:9 There remains a rest for the people of God.

Part of that rest is to cast all your cares upon Him and live by His grace that everything we need is already done and it's on the way; it will manifest as you use your faith in that Jesus has already made a way for you through the power of the work of the cross, and as you believe that you will enjoy life and just rest in Him that it is finished.

Matthew 11:28-29 I will give you rest… You will find rest… For my yoke is easy…

Knowing all we need or ever will need is done causes a supernatural rest a calm a patience to come upon you when you believe it, it also brings about a ceasing from a works mentality.

Some people try so hard to obey God, receive from God all they talk about are spiritual things. They continue to pray something like, what else must I do in order to receive my miracle and they miss out on enjoying life and God's creation because they are so serious. We need to learn to live by the grace of God and that it all has been provided for us, just sit back and enjoy the ride, give it all to Him and then rest.

When we keep trying to get something that means we don't believe it's already done. When we believe it's already done, we will have a rest that is awesome. It's not about your faith, but that He finished all the work on the cross and we just need to accept that, believe that and then rest. When we don't we will get into unbelief and that is not good. So stop working and start resting in Jesus name.

Chapter 17

It is Working

II Corinthians 5:7 We walk by faith and not by sight (or the senses).

Romans 1:17 The righteous shall live by faith.

Faith in God's word and that all he promised is finished, its mine right now by the grace and power of the work of the cross. Faith says it is done not going to be done.

God's grace is greater than our weakness, doubts and sins, so don't get legalistic about faith that you have to be perfect in faith before you will receive that is not true. God's grace makes up the difference and nobody is perfect so quit trying to be perfect. Walking by faith is that you believe all you need in this life Jesus has already provided it for you on the cross and because of His grace He has given it to you as a free inheritance.

Faith calls things done all because Jesus said it is finished. (John 19:30 and Romans 4:17)

We are to have the power of Jesus name at work in us and for us whether we see it or not.

Acts 3:16 His name through faith in His name has made this man well.

Philippians 2: 9-11 At the name of Jesus every knee shall bow…

So we need to believe the power, the glory and the grace that is in that name is at work in my body, marriage, ministry, finances or whatever once you declare it over and into your situation. When you think of your problem just rest in the fact it has to bow to the name of Jesus and then praise Him that you believe it's bowing in Jesus name.

We must believe that the power of the work of the cross is at work in my body, finances, marriage etc., even when you see nothing happening, we must declare I believe the power of the work of the cross is working in Jesus name, and then just enter His rest in Jesus name.

We must continue having faith that His resurrection power is at work in me and for me, even when we don't see it, we must declare our faith that says I believe it's working.

Romans 8:11 The same Spirit that raised Jesus from the dead is making alive (resurrecting) my mortal body…

Philippians 3:10 That I may know Him and the power of his resurrection…

We must continue to believe that the Glory of God is at work even when we don't see it; we must declare it is at work even when we don't see anything.

John 11:40 Did I not say that you would see the glory of God if you believed.

The Glory manifested when Jesus raised Lazarus from the dead, but it was at work before that miracle manifested, so don't get discouraged when you see little or even nothing as God's power is still at work. Remember 2 Kings 6:17 Elisha's servant could not see that the Angels were surrounding them, all he could see was the problem until God opened his eyes, but the truth of the matter is they were there all along even when he could not see them, so it is with us, God is at work on our behalf even when we don't see it so just relax and enjoy life.

We must continue in believing and declaring God's creative word and its power is at work in me in Jesus name, even when it looks like nothing is happening. Just a reminder we don't declare it trying to get it to work, but we declare God's Word from the position it is finished and that it is at work right now in me, for me in Jesus name.

Genesis 1:1 In the beginning God created the heaven and the earth.

John 1:14 His word was made flesh (manifested)…

Matthew 8:5-13 This man took Jesus at his Word once it was spoken, he accepted what He said as a done deal, as he believed Gods spoken Word it created the miracle he needed and Jesus honored this man's faith calling it great. When we accept God's word as a done deal, He too will honor our faith and call it great.

As we continue in believing it is done, God's creative word continues to create what was believed and spoken in Jesus name.

We must continue to believe that the fullness of the power of the blood of Jesus is at work in me and for me even when I do not see anything happening.

Revelation 12:11 They overcame him by the blood of the lamb…

So this tells me that the blood of Jesus has within it overcoming power. It is activated when we believe it and declare it in Jesus name.

Ephesians 1:7 We have redemption through the blood of Jesus.

So all that we are redeemed from and all that we are redeemed into is ours through the blood of Jesus. We must continue to believe it is at work and declare it is finished all because of the redemption that is mine through the power of the Blood of Jesus!

We must continue to believe and declare that my faith in the Son of God and all

He promised is at work even when I don't see anything happening yet.

Mark 11:22-24 Have faith in God that whosoever shall say to this mountain be removed and doubts not but believes the things he says will come to pass he will have whatever he says and whatsoever things you desire believe you have received them(as a done deal, it is finished) you shall have them.

Faith is all about believing it's already done!

We must continue to believe that our angels are at work on our behalf even when we don't see anything happening.

Hebrews 1:14 Are they not all ministering spirits sent to minister to those who are heirs of salvation.

Psalm 103:20 Angels hearken unto the voice of His word.

2 Kings 6:16 Fear not there are more with us than against us.

Verse 17 basically tells us they were surrounded by warring angels ready for battle to keep the men of God safe and so it is with us who believe that His angels are at work for us even when we see nothing happening, something is happening but it is in the spirit realm or the heavenly realm, but none the less something is happening as you continue to believe and declare my miracle, my needs are already provided for, they are finished in Jesus name!

Remember in Daniel chapter 10 an angel revealed to Daniel that as soon as he prayed they went to work on his behalf but it took 21 days to battle through the demonic realm, but as Daniel stood in faith not willing to give up they broke through and so it is with all of us who refuse to give up, we will have the promise in the flesh in Jesus name!

We must continue to believe that God is only good and that His goodness is at work in me and for me even when I feel miserable and even discouraged when it seems like nothing is happening In Jesus name.

Psalm 23:6 Surely goodness and mercy shall follow me all the days of my life.

Psalm 27:13 I had fainted unless I had believed to see the goodness of the Lord in the land of the living.

Even when it seems like God's goodness is a million miles away, we must continue to believe He is good and His goodness is at work on my behalf, we must declare it and praise Him for it.

Faith is believing God's goodness is a done deal and it's at work on your behalf. It takes no faith to declare His goodness when life is great, but it does take faith to declare He is good and I will only accept His goodness when you are in a war zone.

So be strengthened with His might to continue to believe it is finished in Jesus name!

We must continue to believe His love is at work in me and for me even when it looks impossible and you feel anger and disappointment.

John3:16 For God so loved the world…

This means you. One of the tricks of the devil is to get you to doubt just how much He loves us. He does this by getting us to focus on our pain and not His promise.

We must have a greater revelation that God loves me so much He put all my sin, pain, hurts, and sicknesses upon His son so I could be healed. He accepts you just as you are. You do not have to do anything to get Him to love you and accept you. He chose you to be in His family not because of anything except that He loves you.

Ephesians 3:17-18 reveals to us that we need to pray that we would know this unlimited love God has for us, it passes all knowledge and understanding, it cannot be humanly explained, it must be received by faith, accepted and experienced.

Like most people when I got born again the first thing I experienced was an abundance of love. I began to love everybody and everything; I was saturated with love and peace.

It sometimes is very challenging to continue in love when you have made so many mistakes and when others have used and abused you, but we must realize they are not perfect as we are not perfect and we must choose to forgive and be gracious.

The more love we experience the more love we can give, so let's continue believing that no matter what, God loves me this I know, you might need to declare this over your life daily!

His love will withhold no good thing from you!

We must continue to believe and declare that I am delivered from all darkness and oppression of the devil even when darkness and oppression is surrounding me.

Colossians 1:13 He has delivered me from the dominion of darkness and transferred me into the kingdom of His beloved son.

It is real simple. Jesus has already delivered you from all influence of darkness, darkness has no legal right to your life as a believer because Jesus has redeemed you from it, so rise up and say you cannot remain get out in Jesus name, I do not belong to you any longer, Jesus through the finished works on the cross has set me free from you and then just begin to praise the Lord!

We must continue to believe God's power is at work in me and for me even when it looks like it is not working.

Matthew 10:1 He gave his disciples power…

Acts 1:8 You shall receive power after the Holy Spirit has come upon you…

Acts 10:38 How God anointed Jesus with the Holy Spirit and power…

Even though we may not feel it, see it we must continue to believe God's power is at work on my behalf in Jesus name.

Also remember that the blessing of the Lord (proverbs 10:22) and the blessing of Abraham (Galatians 3:13-14) is at work in your life even when it seems nothing is going on because we know it's at work in Jesus name. We know this because Jesus has already provided it for you through the power of the work of the cross. So we need to continue declaring it as if it's already done because it is. I believe it is done and I command it to manifest in Jesus name! Declare boldly!

Chapter 18

New Covenant Praying

The difference between old covenant praying and new covenant praying is that in the old covenant you had to ask and keep on asking for God to do something and then wait to see if he would do it. You would ask today and if you didn't receive it then you would ask every day until you either received it or you just gave up and quit. That also sounds like how a lot of people pray today and that's why many of us are not excited to pray.

To many people teach an old covenant function in prayer thinking its new covenant all because it's in the bible, we need to learn how to pray according to the new covenant and that means we pray from the position it is finished not from a position of asking God to do something he told us to do or that he already made provision and you don't need to ask for something that already belongs to you, all you need to do is accept the fact that it is already done and then command it to manifest by using the authority.

Jesus gave us in the Power of Jesus name. Remember in Acts 3 Peter and John came to a crippled man and notice, they did not ask God to do anything they just prayed in line with the new covenant that Jesus already provided his healing and commanded him to be healed in Jesus name and that is how we are to pray today, with authority and bold power in Jesus name!

John 14:13 Whatever you ask (which means to demand as your legal right) in my name I will do it.

He did not say to ask as if you don't know what he will do, but to demand or command the promise to manifest like Peter did in Acts 3 and like Paul did in Acts 16:16.

To many people are asking God to do something about a problem when He gave us grace and power to use His authority and His Word and pray with authority to receive a miracle.. Before you can function like this you need to know 100% what God's Word says about the problem and what solutions the cross provided for the problem. Once you know those things you can pray and know it is finished no matter what you see or don't see.

So how we intercede for others is not to ask God to do something, but to declare the answer from the beginning that it is finished, problem solved! Not hoping it might be someday but it is done now.

Mark 11:24 Believe you receive… means I believe it is done, not going to be but according to John 19:30 it is finished.

Look at how Jesus prayed for others, He never asked God to do something about their need He just used the grace and power He was given and commanded or demanded things and they all came to pass.

As the revelation of the power of the work of the cross becomes more real to you about all that Jesus did on the cross your whole life will change. You won't work so hard spiritually in prayer, intercession, warfare, you will just rest in the fact that its already done and just go on enjoying life, not always trying to get ahead or trying to get to the next realm in Christ.

Jesus didn't intend for the Christian life to be so hard. He said my yoke is easy and my burden is light. But it is difficult if we have to toil or struggle for every little blessing we get, that's works not grace. Grace is that He provided it all for you just accept it as a done deal and praise Him for the power of the work of the cross.

As you continue in your journey of faith, I pray and impart into you a greater revelation of the Lord Jesus Christ and what He did for you on the cross of Calvary. May the eyes of your understanding be opened in Jesus name. May you see and comprehend the fullness of the finished works of Jesus. I set myself in agreement with you that whatever needs you have in your life, Jesus through the power of the work of the cross has already provided the answers for those needs. I declare they are met in Jesus name.

I say to you, rise up into the fullness of the healed, prosperous, victorious life that Jesus died on the cross for you to have. Every resistance, hindrance to your faith and your walk with Him, I declare broken, destroyed, paralyzed in Jesus name. You are the healed, you are the victorious, you are the prosperous, in Jesus name. God bless you.

www.ingramcontent.com/pod-product-compliance
Lightning Source LLC
Chambersburg PA
CBHW071311060426
42444CB00034B/1958